AIR FRYER COOKBOOK
FOR BEGINNERS
2022

Easy Air Fryer Recipes you
Can Enjoy Cooking in Your Kitchen

Gemma Doe

Table of Contents

Introduction

An air fryer is a new piece of technology that cooks food by circulating hot air around it. It's like the best thing about cooking in a fryer, but without the mess. Air frying gives you crispy, crunchy textures on the outside and tender and moist textures on the inside. And because your food isn't submerged in oil, less fat drips off and stays in your dish!

Air frying also has an energy-saving design that uses up to two-thirds less power than a traditional oven or stovetop cooking. And air frying is a very quick way to whip up a special meal—it's faster and easier than using your oven or stovetop, and it saves you the time of finding an extra pan and pot.

"An air fryer is a kitchen appliance that cooks food by circulating hot air around the foods at high speed and heating the oil. Air frying uses less oil than deep frying, which in turn makes the food healthier to eat."

Benefits of cooking in an air fryer include cooking with less fat, eliminating odor from cooking oils, and not having to deal with messy dishes as it cooks! In addition, the taste is enhanced and the food is crispier because of the air circulation. For a variety of recipes, users can use a source of oil that has a lower burning point than oil used for deep frying.

The air fryer is an ideal kitchen appliance at home for anyone who would like to cut down on saturated fats and calories in their diet. Air fryer cooking helps you to prepare foods with less fat and calories so you can maintain your healthy weight without sacrificing tastiness, texture, or flavor.

An air fryer is an appliance that is becoming popular currently that has become the talk of the town for members of the wellness community. The air fryer lets you cook with less fat and fewer calories. The air fryer contains a basket that comes with a lid, which has a wire mesh to allow maximum airflow while cooking. The nutrition gets circulated in this hot air and gets heated up like in deep frying but not in oil, thereby cooking food without having it to absorb all those extra fats or oils. Air frying cooks food at low temperatures and does not require deep frying so excess oil does not get absorbed by the food that you are cooking. This leads to fewer calories as well as excess fat. This method of cooking is healthier than deep-frying your food. Air frying is best suited for cooking potatoes, sweet potatoes, frozen vegetables, chicken wings, fish fillets, and a variety of other food items.

The air fryer uses hot air to cook your food and it is therefore important to know the temperature setting that you will use as well as the cooking time for your type of food. The temperature settings should be set at 380 degrees F to avoid burning or overcooking the nutrition in your food. You can use an air fryer to prepare a variety of different foods. Some people like to season their food with some sort of herbs and spices before they start using the air fryer. A lot of manufacturers have started producing air fryers, which makes them affordable for everyone

Conversion Table 1

Kitchen Measurement Conversion Tables			
Liquid or Volume Measures (approximate)			
1 teaspoon		1/3 tablespoon	5 ml
1 tablespoon	1/2 fluid ounce	3 teaspoons	15 ml 15 cc
2 tablespoons	1 fluid ounce	1/8 cup, 6 teaspoons	30 ml, 30 cc
1/4 cup	2 fluid ounces	4 tablespoons	59 ml
1/3 cup	2 2/3 fluid ounces	5 tablespoons & 1 teaspoon	79 ml
1/2 cup	4 fluid ounces	8 tablespoons	118 ml
2/3 cup	5 1/3 fluid ounces	10 tablespoons & 2 teaspoons	158 ml
3/4 cup	6 fluid ounces	12 tablespoons	177 ml
7/8 cup	7 fluid ounces	14 tablespoons	207 ml
1 cup	8 fluid ounces/ 1/2 pint	16 tablespoons	237 ml
2 cups	16 fluid ounces/ 1 pint	32 tablespoons	473 ml
4 cups	32 fluid ounces	1 quart	946 ml
1 pint	16 fluid ounces/ 1 pint	32 tablespoons	473 ml
2 pints	32 fluid ounces	1 quart	946 ml 0.946 liters
8 pints	1 gallon/ 128 fluid ounces	4 quarts	3785 ml 3.78 liters
4 quarts	1 gallon/128 fluid ounces	1 gallon	3785 ml 3.78 liters
1 liter	1.057 quarts		1000 ml
1 gallon	4 quarts	128 fluid ounces	3785 ml 3.78 liters

Conversion Table 2

MATH CONVERSION CHART – LIQUID VOLUME (US)

Please note that these conversions work for US liquids only!

METRIC CONVERSIONS					
1 centiliter	=	10 milliliters	1 cl	=	10 ml
1 liter	=	1000 milliliters	1 l	=	1000 ml

STANDARD CONVERSIONS					
1 tablespoon	=	3 teaspoons	1 Tbsp	=	3 tsp
1 fluid ounce	=	2 tablespoons	1 fl oz	=	2 Tbsp
1 fluid ounce	=	8 drams	1 fl oz	=	8 drams
1 gill	=	4 fluid ounces	1 gi	=	4 fl oz
1 cup	=	8 fluid ounces	1 cup	=	8 fl oz
1 pint	=	2 cups	1 pt	=	2 cups
1 pint	=	16 fluid ounces	1 pt	=	16 fl oz
1 quart	=	2 pints	1 qt	=	2 pt
1 gallon	=	4 quarts	1 gal	=	4 qt
1 gallon	=	128 fluid ounces	1 gal	=	128 fl oz

1 gallon = 4 quarts = 8 pints = 16 cups = 128 fluid ounces

METRIC -> STANDARD CONVERSIONS					
1 milliliter	=	0.033814 fluid ounces	1 ml	=	0.033814 fl oz
1 liter	=	33.814022 fluid ounces	1 l	=	33.814022 fl oz
1 liter	=	2.113376 pints	1 l	=	2.113376 pints

STANDARD -> METRIC CONVERSIONS					
1 fluid ounce	=	29.57353 milliliters	1 fl oz	=	29.57353 ml
1 pint	=	473.17648 milliliters	1 pt	=	473.17648 ml
1 pint	=	0.47318 liters	1 pt	=	0.47318 l
1 gallon, liquid	=	3.7854 liters	1 gallon	=	3.7854 l

Breakfast

Cheesy Bacon and Fried Eggs

Preparation time: 15 minutes
Cooking time: 15 minutes
Servings: 4

Ingredients:

- Salt
- 2 cup baby spinach
- Pepper
- 4 bacon slices
- ½ cup divided shredded cheddar cheese
- 4 eggs
- 1 tbsp. extra-virgin olive oil

Directions

1. Melt the oil in a pan over medium-high flame. Put the spinach and cook until wilted. Transfer to a plate and drain excess liquid. Transfer them into 4 greased ramekins.
2. Add a slice of bacon and egg to each ramekin. Sprinkle cheese on top then some seasonings.
3. Arrange the ramekins inside the cooking basket of the Air Fryer.
4. Cook for 15 minutes at 350 degrees Fahrenheit.

Nutrition:

Calories 256 Carbs 1.4g Protein 16.5g

Air-Fried Blueberry Bagels

Preparation time: 10 minutes
Cooking time: 10 minutes
Servings: 2

Ingredients:

- 1 tbsp. water
- ¾ cup self-rising flour
- ½ cup dried blueberries
- 1 egg
- ½ cup plain Greek yogurt
- 1 tbsp. melted butter

Directions

1. Combine the yogurt and flour in a mixing bowl. Stir together with a wooden spoon until a tacky dough forms.
2. Transfer to a lightly floured flat work surface, and roll the dough into a ball.
3. Flatten the dough slightly, and sprinkle the dried blueberries on top.
4. Knead the dough to work in the blueberries throughout.
5. Cut the dough into 2 pieces, and roll each piece into a log. Form each log into a bagel shape, pinching the ends together.
6. Combine the water and egg in a sizable bowl to whisk well.
7. Place the bagels in the fryer basket, and brush with the prepared egg wash.
8. Bake for 10 minutes at 330 degrees Fahrenheit
9. Remove from the air fryer, brush with the melted butter, and serve warm.

Nutrition:

Calories 182 Carbs 16g Protein 10g

Morning Sandwich Cheesy Stuffed

Preparation time: 1 minute
Cooking time: 8 minutes
Servings: 2

Ingredients:

- 1 tbsp. butter
- 4 frozen bread slices
- 2 cheddar cheese slices

Directions

1. Evenly spread butter on each bread slice evenly.

2. Place one cheese slice between two bread slices.

3. Preheat your Air Fryer to a temperature of 360 degrees Fahrenheit.

4. Transfer sandwiches into fryer basket and let them cook for 8 minutes.

5. Serve with coffee or tea, or with vegetables.

Nutrition:

Calories 272 Carbs 20.37g Protein 10.39g

Mushroom, Tomato Frittata

Preparation time: 3 minutes
Cooking time: 15 minutes
Servings: 2

Ingredients:

- ¼ cup chopped onion
- 1 cubed bell peppers
- 1 tbsp. chopped chives
- ½ cup sliced mushrooms
- 4 eggs
- ¼ cup milk
- Salt
- ¼ cup grated parmesan cheese
- Pepper
- 6 halved Cherry tomatoes

Directions
1. Preheat your Air Fryer to a temperature of 325 degrees Fahrenheit (160 degrees Celsius).
2. Take a bowl and whisk eggs for 1-2 minutes.
3. Season with salt nd pepper.
4. Add in onion, chives, cheese, bell peppers, tomatoes, and mushrooms and mix.
5. Transfer mixture into a baking pan that can fit into Air Fryer basket and cook for 15 minutes.

Nutrition:

Calories 245 Carbs 14.59g Protein 17.89g

French toast Sticks

Preparation time: 5 minutes
Cooking time: 15 minutes
Servings: 12

Ingredients:

- 1 tsp. vanilla extract
- 1 tbsp. butter
- 1 tsp. ground cinnamon
- 1 egg
- 1 tsp. stevia
- ¼ cup milk
- Cooking oil
- 4 slices Texas toast

Directions

1. Divide the bread slices into 3 pieces each.
2. Place the butter in a small, microwave-safe bowl.
3. Set in the microwave for 15 seconds, or until the butter has melted.
4. Remove the bowl from the microwave. Add the egg, stevia, cinnamon, milk, and vanilla extract. Whisk until fully combined.
5. Spray the cooking basket with cooking oil.
6. Dredge each of the bread sticks in the egg mixture.
7. Place the French toast sticks in the air fryer. It is okay to stack them. Spray the French toast sticks with cooking oil. Cook for 8 minutes at 375 degrees Fahrenheit.
8. Open the air fryer and flip each of the French toast sticks.
9. Allow to cook until the French toast sticks are crisp.
10. Cool before serving.

Nutrition:

Calories 152 Carbohydrates 7g Protein 2g

Grilled Ham and Cheese

Preparation time: 5 minutes
Cooking time: 10 minutes
Servings: 2

Ingredients:

- 4 slices smoked country ham
- 4 slices bread
- 4 thick slices tomato
- 1 tsp. butter
- 4 slices Cheddar cheese

Directions

1. Spread ½ tsp. of butter onto one side of 2 slices of bread. Each sandwich will have 1 slice of bread with butter and 1 slice without.
2. Assemble each sandwich by layering 2 slices of ham, 2 slices of cheese, and 2 slices of tomato on the unbuttered pieces of bread. Top with the other bread slices, buttered side up.
3. Place the sandwiches in the air fryer buttered-side down. Cook for 4 minutes.
4. Open the air fryer. Flip the grilled cheese sandwiches. Cook for an additional 4 minutes.
5. Cool before serving.
6. Cut each sandwich in half and enjoy.

Nutrition:
Calories 525 Carbs 34g Protein 41g

Vegetable Egg Cups

Preparation Time: 10 minutes
Cooking time: 20 minutes
Servings: 4

Ingredients:

- 4 eggs
- 1 tbsp. cilantro, chopped
- 4 tbsp. half and half
- 1 cup cheddar cheese, shredded
- 1 cup vegetables, diced
- Pepper
- Salt

Directions

1. Spray four ramekins with cooking spray and set aside.

2. In a mixing bowl, whisk eggs with cilantro, half and half, vegetables, 1/2 cup cheese, pepper, and salt.

3. Pour egg mixture into the four ramekins.

4. Place ramekins in air fryer basket and cook at 300 degrees Fahrenheit for 12 minutes.

5. Top with remaining 1/2 cup cheese and cook for 2 minutes more at 400 degrees Fahrenheit.

Nutrition:

Calories 194 Carbs 6g Protein 13g

Spinach Frittata

Preparation Time: 5 minutes
Cooking time: 8 minutes
Servings: 1

Ingredients:

- 3 eggs
- 1 cup spinach, chopped
- 1 small onion, minced
- 2 tbsp. mozzarella cheese, grated
- Pepper
- Salt

Directions

1. Preheat the air fryer to 350 degrees Fahrenheit.

2. Spray air fryer pan with cooking spray.

3. In a bowl, whisk eggs with remaining ingredients until well combined.

4. Pour egg mixture into the prepared pan and place pan in the air fryer basket.

5. Cook frittata for 8 minutes or until set.

Nutrition:

Calories 384 Carbs 10.7g Protein 34.3g

Omelette Frittata

Preparation Time: 10 minutes
Cooking time: 6 minutes
Servings: 2

Ingredients:

- 3 eggs, lightly beaten
- 2 tbsp. cheddar cheese, shredded
- 2 tbsp. heavy cream
- 2 mushrooms, sliced
- 1/4 small onion, chopped
- 1/4 bell pepper, diced
- Pepper
- Salt

Directions

1. In a bowl, whisk eggs with cream, vegetables, pepper, and salt.
2. Preheat the air fryer to 380 degrees Fahrenheit.
3. Pour egg mixture into the air fryer pan. Place pan in air fryer basket and cook for 5 minutes.
4. Add shredded cheese on top of the frittata and cook for 1 minute more.

Nutrition:

Calories 160 Carbs 4g Protein 12g

Simple Egg Soufflé

Preparation Time: 5 minutes
Cooking time: 8 minutes
Servings: 2

Ingredients:

- 2 eggs
- 1/4 tsp. chili pepper
- 2 tbsp. heavy cream
- 1/4 tsp. pepper
- 1 tbsp. parsley, chopped
- Salt

Directions

1. In a bowl, whisk eggs with remaining gradients.

2. Spray two ramekins with cooking spray.

3. Pour egg mixture into the prepared ramekins and place into the air fryer basket.

4. Cook soufflé at 380 degrees Fahrenheit for 8 minutes.

Nutrition:

Calories 116 Carbs 1.1g Protein 6g

Vegetable Egg Soufflé

Preparation Time: 10 minutes
Cooking time: 20 minutes
Servings: 4

Ingredients:

- 4 large eggs
- 1 tsp. onion powder
- 1 tsp. garlic powder
- 1 tsp. red pepper, crushed
- 1/2 cup broccoli florets, chopped
- 1/2 cup mushrooms, chopped

Directions

1. Spray four ramekins with cooking spray and set aside.

2. In a bowl, whisk eggs with onion powder, garlic powder, and red pepper.

3. Add mushrooms and broccoli and stir well.

4. Pour egg mixture into the prepared ramekins and place ramekins into the air fryer basket.

5. Cook at 350 degrees Fahrenheit for 15 minutes. Make sure soufflé is cooked if soufflé is not cooked then cook for 5 minutes more.

Nutrition:

Calories 91 Carbs 4.7g Protein 7.4g

Zucchini Muffins

Preparation Time: 10 minutes
Cooking time: 20 minutes
Servings: 8

Ingredients:

- 6 eggs
- 4 drops stevia
- 1/4 cup Swerve
- 1/3 cup coconut oil, melted
- 1 cup zucchini, grated
- 3/4 cup coconut flour
- 1/4 tsp. ground nutmeg
- 1 tsp. ground cinnamon
- 1/2 tsp. baking soda

Directions

1. Preheat the air fryer to 325 degrees Fahrenheit.
2. Add all ingredients except zucchini in a bowl and mix well.
3. Add zucchini and stir well.
4. Pour batter into the silicone muffin molds and place into the air fryer basket.
5. Cook muffins for 20 minutes.

Nutrition:

Calories 136 Carbs 1g Protein 4g

Jalapeno Breakfast Muffins

Preparation Time: 10 minutes
Cooking time: 15 minutes
Servings: 8

Ingredients:

- 5 eggs
- 1/3 cup coconut oil, melted
- 2 tsp. baking powder
- 3 tbsp. erythritol
- 3 tbsp. jalapenos, sliced
- 1/4 cup unsweetened coconut milk
- 2/3 cup coconut flour
- 3/4 tsp. sea salt

Directions

1. Preheat the air fryer to 325 degrees Fahrenheit.

2. In a large bowl, stir together coconut flour, baking powder, erythritol, and sea salt.

3. Stir in eggs, jalapenos, coconut milk, and coconut oil until well combined.

4. Pour batter into the silicone muffin molds and place into the air fryer basket.

5. Cook muffins for 15 minutes.

Nutrition:

Calories 125 Carbs 7g Protein 3g

Lunch

Chicken Parmesan

Preparation Time: 7 minutes
Cooking Time: 9 minutes
Servings: 5

Ingredients:

- 4 thin chicken breast cutlets
- 2 tbsp. Parmesan cheese grated
- 5 tbsp. of seasoned breadcrumbs
- 1 tbsp. olive oil
- ½ cup marinara sauce
- 6 tbsp. mozzarella cheese

Directions

1. Preheat the Air Fryer to 360 degrees F.
2. Combine the Parmesan cheese and breadcrumbs in a bowl.
3. Brush the chicken with the olive oil then dip into the bread crumb mixture.
4. Place the chicken breasts into the air fryer basket and cook for 6 minutes.
5. Top each chicken breast piece with marinara sauce and mozzarella cheese. Cook for 3 more minutes or until the cheese has melted.
6. Serve warm.

Nutrition:

Calories 272 kcal Carbs 5.5 g Protein 30.7 g.

Air Fried Hot Dogs

Preparation Time: 2 minutes
Cooking Time: 5 minutes
Servings: 4

Ingredients:

- 4 hot dogs
- 4 hot dog buns

Directions

1. Preheat the Air Fryer to 380 degrees F and place the hot dogs on the center rack of the air fryer. Air fry for 5 minutes.
2. Remove the hot dog and place into the sliced hot dog bun. Add desired toppings. If you added cheese, place the hot dog into the air fryer for 2 more minutes. Serve.

Nutrition:

Calories 177 kcal Carbs 27.2 g Protein 9.3 g.

Popcorn Chicken

Preparation Time: 10 minutes
Cooking Time: 8 minutes
Servings: 3
Ingredients:

- 3 chicken breasts, cut into equal sized cubes
- ½ cup buttermilk
- ¼ cup cornstarch
- 2 cups corn flakes cereal, finely crushed
- ¼ tsp. garlic powder
- ¼ tsp. onion powder
- ¼ tsp. paprika
- Salt and pepper to taste

Directions

1. Preheat the Air Fryer to 380 degrees F.
2. Place the buttermilk, corn starch and corn flakes in separate bowls for coating the chicken.
3. Coat each piece of chicken first in corn starch, then in buttermilk and finally in the corn flakes crumbs before placing in the air fryer basket. Cook for 8 minutes. Serve with ketchup or your favorite dipping sauce.

Nutrition:

Calories 392 kcal Carbs 28.2 g Protein 43.3 g.

Bacon-Wrapped Scallions

Preparation Time: 9 minutes
Cooking Time: 8 minutes
Servings: 4

Ingredients:

- 8 large scallops, cleaned
- 4 pieces bacon, cut down the center lengthwise
- Olive oil
- Salt and pepper to taste

Directions

1. Preheat the Air Fryer to 380 degrees F.

2. Remove any side muscles from the scallops and pat dry with paper towels.

3. Wrap each scallop in a piece of bacon and secure with a toothpick.

4. Coat the scallops with olive oil then season with salt and pepper.

5. Place the scallops in a single layer in the air fryer basket and cook for 8 minutes. Flip halfway through the cooking process.

6. Serve warm.

Nutrition:

Calories171 kcal Carbs 1.7 g Protein 17.1 g

Breaded Catfish

Preparation Time: 8 minutes
Cooking Time: 8 minutes
Servings: 5

Ingredients:

- 4 catfish fillets
- ½ cup seasoned breadcrumbs
- ½ cup all-purpose flour
- 1 egg, beaten
- Salt and pepper to taste

Directions:

1. Preheat the Air Fryer 380 degrees F.

2. Toss the catfish with flour to coat.

3. Coat in the beaten egg.

4. Dredge in the breadcrumbs.

5. Place in the air fryer basket and air fry for 8 minutes.

6. Sprinkle with salt and pepper and serve.

Nutrition:

Calories 344 kcal Carbs 20.5 g Protein 29.4 g.

Baked Potato

Preparation Time: 3 minutes
Cooking Time: 40 minutes
Servings: 2

Ingredients:

- 2 Russet potatoes
- 1 tbsp. olive oil
- 1 tsp. parsley, chopped
- 1 garlic clove, minced
- Salt and pepper to taste

Directions

1. Preheat the Air Fryer to 380 degrees F.
2. Wash and dry the potatoes.
3. Prick the potatoes all over with a fork to create holes.
4. Mix the rest of the ingredients together in a small bowl then rub the mixture over the potatoes.
5. Air fry the potatoes for 40 minutes or until fork tender.
6. Plate the potatoes, slice down the center and top with desired items.

Nutrition:

Calories: 210 kcal Carbs 34 g Protein 3.7 g.

Cajun Shrimp

Preparation Time: 5 minutes
Cooking Time: 8 minutes
Servings: 5

Ingredients:

- 1 lb. jumbo shrimp, cleaned and peeled
- 1 tbsp. Cajun seasoning
- 1 red bell pepper, sliced
- 1 tbsp. olive oil

Directions

1. Preheat the Air Fryer to 380 degrees F.
2. Combine all the ingredients in a large bowl and toss so that the shrimp is thoroughly coated in the seasoning.
3. Transfer the mixture to the air fryer basket and cook for 8 minutes. Stir the basket three times.
4. Serve with desired sides.

Nutrition:

Calories 96 kcal Carbs 1.8 g Protein 16.5 g

Ranch Cod Fillet

Preparation Time: 8 minutes
Cooking Time: 12 minutes
Servings: 4

Ingredients:

- 4 cod fillets
- ½ cup panko bread crumbs
- 1 packet dry ranch seasoning mix
- 2 eggs, beaten
- 2 tbsp. olive oil

Directions

1. Preheat the Air Fryer to 380 degrees F.
2. Mix the olive oil, breadcrumbs and ranch seasoning mix until a loose and crumbly mixture is formed.
3. Dip the cod fillets into the egg and then into the bread crumb mixture to coat thoroughly.
4. Place the cod fillets into the air fryer basket and cook for 12 minutes.
5. Garnish and serve.

Nutrition:

Calories 236 kcal Carbs 9.9 g Protein: 24.6 g.

Pepperoni Pizza

Preparation Time: 10 minutes
Cooking Time: 10 minutes
Servings: 4

Ingredients:

- 8-oz pizza dough
- ½ tbsp. olive oil
- ¼ cup pizza sauce
- ½ cup mozzarella cheese
- ¼ cup pepperoni

Directions

1. Preheat the Air Fryer to 380 degrees F.
2. Roll out the pizza dough in an 8" circle on a clean, floured surface with floured hands.
3. Brush the pizza with the olive oil and layer the pizza sauce, cheese and pepperoni on the dough in that order. Ensure that a border of ½ inch is left uncovered around the pizza.
4. Air fry fo10 minutes or the cheese has melted and the crusted is golden brown.
5. Remove the pizza from the air fryer, garnish as desired, slice and serve.

Nutrition:

Calories 368 kcal Carbs 25.9 g Protein 7.6 g.

Succulent Turkey Breast

Preparation Time: 5 minutes
Cooking Time: 30 minutes
Servings: 4

Ingredients:

- 2 lb. turkey breast
- ½ tbsp. all-purpose seasoning
- Olive oil
- Salt and pepper to taste

Directions

1. Preheat the Air Fryer to 350 degrees F.
2. Coat the turkey in the olive oil and season with the remaining ingredients.
3. Place the turkey into the air fryer basket skin side down and cook for 30 minutes. Flip half way through. The turkey will have an internal temperature of 160 degrees F when it is done. Allow the turkey to rest for 10 minutes before serving.

Nutrition:

Calories 266 kcal Carbs: 9.6 g Protein 38.7 g.

Turkey Burger

Preparation Time: 5 minutes
Cooking Time: 10 minutes
Servings: 4

Ingredients:

- 1 lb. ground turkey
- 1 tbsp. soy sauce
- Salt and pepper to taste
- 2 garlic cloves, minced
- 4 hamburger buns, halved and toasted
- Lettuce
- Tomatoes
- Red onions, thinly sliced
- Low-fat mayo

Directions:

1. Preheat the Air Fryer to 375 degrees F and spray a small baking sheet with nonstick spray.
2. Combine the turkey, soy sauce and garlic in a large bowl.
3. Shape the mixture into 4 patties. Flatten to ½" inch thick circles. Season the patties with salt and pepper.
4. Air fry for 10 minutes. Flip the patties halfway through the process.
5. Spread mayo onto the hamburger buns. Place lettuce on one side then layer with the patties and veggies. Cover with the other bun slice and serve.

Nutrition:

Calories 369 kcal Carbs 27.1 g Protein 36.1 g.

Simple Citrus Salmon

Preparation Time: 7 minutes
Cooking Time: 8 minutes
Servings: 4

Ingredients:

- 4 fresh salmon fillets
- 1 large lemon
- ½ tsp. paprika
- Salt and pepper to taste

Directions

1. Preheat the Air Fryer to 375 degrees F.

2. Season the salmon with all of the spices.

3. Slice lemons thinly and evenly divide the slices by placing them on top of the salmon pieces

4. Place the salmon pieces in an even layer in the air fryer basket and cook for 8 minutes. The salmon is done when it reaches an internal temperature of 145 degrees F at the thickest part of the meat.

5. Garnish as desired and serve.

Nutrition:

Calories 240 kcal Carbs 1.5 g Protein 34.7 g.

Air Fryer Oysters

Preparation Time: 9 minutes
Cooking Time: 2 minutes
Servings: 3

Ingredients:

- 12 fresh oysters, shucked
- 2 large eggs, beaten
- 1 cup seasoned breadcrumbs
- ½ cup all-purpose flour
- Olive oil
- Salt and pepper to taste

Directions:

1. Preheat the Air Fryer to 400 degrees F.

2. Place the beaten egg in one bowl, the flour in another and finally, the bread crumbs in a shallow bowl.

3. Bread the oysters by first dipping them into the flour then the egg and finally, the breadcrumbs.

4. Line the oysters in a single layer in the air fryer basket. Spray with olive oil. Cook for 2 minutes. Stir the oysters at the 1 minute mark.

5. Sprinkle with salt and pepper and serve.

Nutrition:

Calories 377 kcal Carbs 41.5 g Protein 17 g.

Rotisserie Chicken Salad

Preparation Time: 15 minutes
Cooking Time: 20 minutes
Servings: 8

Ingredients:

- 1 whole chicken, cut into 8 pieces
- 1 tsp. garlic powder
- 1 tsp. onion powder
- 1 tsp. paprika
- 1 tsp. dried oregano
- 1 tsp. dried thyme
- Veggie mix, cooked
- Salt and pepper to taste

Directions

1. Preheat the Air Fryer to 350 degrees F.
2. Combine all the spices then sprinkle over the chicken. Rub the seasoning into the chicken.
3. Place the chicken in the air fryer basket for 20 minutes. Flip halfway through the process. Ensure that the chicken has reached an internal temperature of 165 degrees before serving. Serve with steamed or sautéed veggies. Top with desired sauce.

Nutrition:

Calories 41 kcal Carbs 1.5 g Protein 5.6 g.

Maple-Flavored Salmon

Preparation Time: 15 minutes
Cooking Time: 12 minutes
Servings: 4

Ingredients:

- 4 fresh salmon fillets
- 2 tbsp. of maple syrup
- 3 tbsp. soy sauce
- 1 tbsp. sriracha hot sauce
- 1 garlic clove, minced

Directions

1. Combine all ingredients in a sealable plastic bag. Allow the salmon to marinate for at least 30 minutes.
2. Preheat the Air Fryer to 400 degrees F.
3. Remove the salmon from the marinade and pat dry before placing in the air fryer basket. Cook for 8 minutes.
4. While the salmon cooks, place the marinade into a small saucepan over medium heat on the stove top. Cook for 1-2 minutes to reduce the sauce.
5. Glaze the sauce over the salmon pieces and serve.

Nutrition:

Calories 269 kcal Fat 11 g Protein 35.3 g.

Dinner

Pork Chops with Broccoli

Preparation time: 15 minutes
Cooking Time: 13 minutes
Servings: 2

Ingredients:

- 2 (5 ounces) bone-in pork chops
- 2 tablespoons avocado oil
- 1/2 teaspoon paprika
- 1/2 teaspoon onion powder
- ½ teaspoon garlic powder
- 1 teaspoon salt
- 2 cups broccoli florets
- 2 garlic cloves, minced

Directions:

1. Rub the pork chops with avocado oil, garlic, paprika, and spices.
2. Add pork chop to the Zone 1 basket of the Air fryer.
3. Return the Air Fryer Basket to the Air Fryer.
4. Choose the Air Fryer mode for Zone 1 with 400 degrees F temperature and 12 minutes cooking time.
5. Add the broccoli to the Zone 2 basket and return it to the unit.
6. Choose the Air Fryer mode for Zone 2 with 375 degrees F temperature and 13 minutes cooking time.
7. Press the SMART FINISH button to sync the settings with Zone 2.
8. Initiate cooking by pressing the START/PAUSE BUTTON.
9. Flip the pork once cooked halfway through.
10. Cut the hardened butter into the cubes and place them on top of the pork chops.
11. Serve warm with crispy broccoli florets

Nutrition:

Calories 410 kcalCarbs 21g Protein 38.4g

Gochujang Brisket

Preparation time: 20 minutes
Cooking Time: 55 minutes
Servings: 6

Ingredients:

- ½ tablespoons sweet paprika
- ½ teaspoon toasted sesame oil
- 2 lbs. beef brisket, cut into 4 pieces
- Salt, to taste
- 1/8 cup Gochujang, Korean chili paste
- Black pepper, to taste
- 1 small onion, diced
- 2 garlic cloves, minced
- 1 teaspoon Asian fish sauce
- 1 ½ tablespoons peanut oil, as needed
- ½ tablespoons fresh ginger, grated
- ¼ teaspoons red chili flakes
- ½ cup of water
- 1 tablespoon ketchup
- 1 tablespoon soy sauce

Directions

1. Thoroughly rub the beef brisket with olive oil, paprika, chili flakes, black pepper, and salt.
2. Cut the brisket in half, then divide the beef in the two Air Fryer baskets.
3. Return the Air Fryer Baskets to the Air Fryer.

4. Choose the Air Fryer mode for Zone 1 with 380 degrees F temperature and 35 minutes cooking time.

5. Select the "MATCH COOK" option to copy the settings for Zone 2.

6. Initiate cooking by pressing the START/PAUSE BUTTON.

7. Flip the brisket halfway through, and resume cooking.

8. Meanwhile, heat oil in a skillet and add ginger, onion, and garlic.

9. Sauté for 5 minutes, then add all the remaining ingredients.

10. Cook the mixture for 15 minutes approximately until well thoroughly mixed.

11. Serve the brisket with this sauce on top.

Nutrition:

Calories 374 kcal Carbs 7.3g Protein 12.3g

Crusted Chicken Breast

Preparation time: 15 minutes
Cooking Time: 28 minutes
Servings: 4

Ingredients:

- 2 large eggs, beaten
- 1/2 cup all-purpose flour
- 1 1/4 cup panko bread crumbs
- 2/3 cup Parmesan, grated
- 4 teaspoons lemon zest
- 2 teaspoons dried oregano
- Salt, to taste
- 1 teaspoon cayenne pepper
- Freshly black pepper, to taste
- 4 boneless skinless chicken breasts

Directions:

1. Beat eggs in one shallow bowl and spread flour in another shallow bowl.

2. Mix panko with oregano, lemon zest, Parmesan, cayenne, oregano, salt, and black pepper in another shallow bowl.

3. First, coat the chicken with flour first, then dip it in the eggs and coat them with panko mixture.

4. Arrange the prepared chicken in the two Air Fryer Baskets.

5. Return the Air Fryer Baskets to the Air Fryer.

6. Choose the Air Fryer mode for Zone 1 with 390 degrees F temperature and 28 minutes cooking time.

7. Select the "MATCH COOK" option to copy the settings for Zone 2.

8. Initiate cooking by pressing the START/PAUSE BUTTON.

9. Flip the half-cooked chicken and continue cooking for 5 minutes until golden.

10. Serve warm

Nutrition:

Calories 220 kcal Carbs 0.9g Protein 25.6g

Sweet Chicken Kabobs

Preparation Time: 20 minutes
Cooking Time: 14 minutes
Servings: 3

Ingredients:

- 4 scallions, chopped
- 2 teaspoons sesame seeds, toasted
- 1 pound chicken tenders
- Wooden skewers, pres oaked
- 1 tablespoon fresh ginger, finely grated
- 4 garlic cloves, minced
- ½ cup pineapple juice
- ½ cup soy sauce
- ¼ cup sesame oil
- A pinch of black pepper

Directions:

1. Preheat the Air fryer to 380 degrees F and grease an Air fryer pan.
2. Mix scallion, ginger, garlic, pineapple juice, soy sauce, oil, sesame seeds, and black pepper in a large baking dish.
3. Thread chicken tenders onto pre-soaked wooden skewers.
4. Coat the skewers generously with marinade and refrigerate for about 2 hours.
5. Transfer half of the skewers in the Air fryer pan and cook for about 7 minutes.
6. Repeat with the remaining mixture and dish out to serve warm.

Nutrition:

Calories 392 kcal Carbs 9.9g Protein 35.8g

Chicken with Apple

Preparation Time: 10 minutes
Cooking Time: 20 minutes
Servings: 8

Ingredients:

- 1 shallot, thinly sliced
- 1 teaspoon fresh thyme, minced
- 2: 4-ouncesboneless, skinless chicken thighs, sliced into chunks
- 1 large apple, cored and cubed
- 1 tablespoon fresh ginger, finely grated
- ½ cup apple cider
- 2 tablespoons maple syrup
- Salt and black pepper, as required

Directions:

1. Preheat the Air fryer to 380 degrees F and grease an Air fryer basket.
2. Mix the shallot, ginger, thyme, apple cider, maple syrup, salt, and black pepper in a bowl.
3. Coat the chicken generously with the marinade and refrigerate to marinate for about 8 hours.
4. Arrange the chicken pieces and cubed apples into the Air Fryer basket and cook for about 20 minutes, flipping once halfway.
5. Dish out the chicken mixture into a serving bowl to serve.

Nutrition:

Calories 299 Kcal Carbs 39.9g Protein26.2g

Chicken with Carrots

Preparation Time: 15 minutes
Cooking Time: 25 minutes
Servings: 2

- Ingredients:

    - 1 carrot, peeled and thinly sliced
    - 2 tablespoons butter
    - 2: 4-ounceschicken breast halves
    - 1 tablespoon fresh rosemary, chopped
    - Salt and black pepper, as required
    - 2 tablespoons fresh lemon juice

Directions:

1. Preheat the Air fryer to 375 degrees F and grease an Air fryer basket.

2. Place 2 square-shaped parchment papers onto a smooth surface and arrange carrot slices evenly in the center of each parchment paper.

3. Drizzle ½ tablespoon of butter over carrot slices and season with salt and black pepper.

4. Layer with chicken breasts and top with rosemary, lemon juice and remaining butter.

5. Fold the parchment paper on all sides and transfer into the Air fryer.

6. Cook for about 25 minutes and dish out in a serving platter to serve.

Nutrition:

Calories 339 kcal Carbs 4.4g Proteins 33.4g

Citrus Turkey Legs

Preparation Time: 15 minutes
Cooking Time: 30 minutes
Servings: 2

Ingredients:

- 1 tablespoon fresh rosemary, minced
- 2 turkey legs
- 2 garlic cloves, minced
- 1 teaspoon fresh lime zest, finely grated
- 2 tablespoons olive oil
- 1 tablespoon fresh lime juice
- Salt and black pepper, as required

Directions

1. Preheat the Air fryer to 350 degrees F and grease an Air fryer basket.

2. Mix the garlic, rosemary, lime zest, oil, lime juice, salt, and black pepper in a bowl.

3. Coat the turkey legs with marinade and refrigerate to marinate for about 8 hours.

4. Arrange the turkey legs into the Air Fryer basket and cook for about 30 minutes, flipping once in between.

5. Dish out the turkey legs into serving plates.

Nutrition:

Calories 458 kcal Carbs 2.3g Protein 44.6g

Simple Turkey Breast

Preparation Time: 20 minutes
Cooking Time: 40 minutes
Servings: 10

Ingredients:

- 1: 8-poundsbone-in turkey breast
- Salt and black pepper, as required
- 2 tablespoons olive oil

Directions

1. Preheat the Air fryer to 360 degrees F and grease an Air fryer basket.
2. Season the turkey breast with salt and black pepper and drizzle with oil.
3. Arrange the turkey breast into the Air Fryer basket, skin side down and cook for about 20 minutes.
4. Flip the side and cook for another 20 minutes.
5. Dish out in a platter and cut into desired size slices to serve.

Nutrition:

Calories 719 kcal Carbs: 4.3g Protein: 97.2g

Delightful Turkey Wings

Preparation Time: 10 minutes
Cooking Time: 26 minutes
Servings: 4

Ingredients:

- 2 pounds turkey wings
- 4 tablespoons chicken rub
- 3 tablespoons olive oil

Directions

1. Preheat the Air fryer to 380 degrees F and grease an Air fryer basket.

2. Mix the turkey wings, chicken rub, and olive oil in a bowl until well combined.

3. Arrange the turkey wings into the Air fryer basket and cook for about 26 minutes, flipping once in between.

4. Dish out the turkey wings in a platter and serve hot.

Nutrition:

Calories 204 kcal Carbs 3g Protein 12g

Buttered Duck Breasts

Preparation Time: 15 minutes
Cooking Time: 22 minutes
Servings: 4

Ingredients:

- 2: 12-ouncesduck breasts
- 3 tablespoons unsalted butter, melted
- Salt and ground black pepper, as required
- ½ teaspoon dried thyme, crushed
- ¼ teaspoon star anise powder

Directions:

1. Preheat the Air fryer to 380 degrees F and grease an Air fryer basket.

2. Season the duck breasts generously with salt and black pepper.

3. Arrange the duck breasts into the prepared Air fryer basket and cook for about 10 minutes.

4. Dish out the duck breasts and drizzle with melted butter.

5. Season with thyme and star anise powder and place the duck breasts again into the Air fryer basket.

6. Cook for about 12 more minutes and dish out to serve warm.

Nutrition:

Calories 296 kcal Carbs 0.1g Protein: 37.5g

Herbed Duck Legs

Preparation Time: 10 minutes
Cooking Time: 30 minutes
Servings: 2

Ingredients:

- ½ tablespoon fresh thyme, chopped
- ½ tablespoon fresh parsley, chopped
- 2 duck legs
- 1 garlic clove, minced
- 1 teaspoon five spice powder
- Salt and black pepper, as required

Directions

1. Preheat the Air fryer to 340 degrees F and grease an Air fryer basket.

2. Mix the garlic, herbs, five spice powder, salt, and black pepper in a bowl.

3. Rub the duck legs with garlic mixture generously and arrange into the Air fryer basket.

4. Cook for about 25 minutes and set the Air fryer to 390 degrees F.

5. Cook for 5 more minutes and dish out to serve hot.

Nutrition:

Calories 138 kcal Carbs 1g Protein 25g

Chicken Wings with Prawn Paste

Preparation Time: 20 minutes
Cooking Time: 8 minutes
Servings: 6

Ingredients:

- Corn flour, as required
- 2 pounds mid-joint chicken wings
- 2 tablespoons prawn paste
- 4 tablespoons olive oil
- 1½ teaspoons sugar
- 2 teaspoons sesame oil
- 1 teaspoon Shaoxing wine
- 2 teaspoons fresh ginger juice

Directions:

1. Preheat the Air fryer to 360 degrees F and grease an Air fryer basket.
2. Mix all the ingredients in a bowl except wings and corn flour.
3. Rub the chicken wings generously with marinade and refrigerate overnight.
4. Coat the chicken wings evenly with corn flour and keep aside.
5. Set the Air fryer to 390 degrees F and arrange the chicken wings in the Air fryer basket.
6. Cook for about 8 minutes and dish out to serve hot.

Nutrition:

Calories 416 kcal Carbs 11.2g Protein 24.4g

Spicy Green Crusted Chicken

Preparation Time: 10 minutes
Cooking Time: 40 minutes
Servings: 6

Ingredients:

- 6 eggs, beaten
- 6 teaspoons parsley
- 4 teaspoons thyme
- 1 pound chicken pieces
- 6 teaspoons oregano
- Salt and freshly ground black pepper, to taste
- 4 teaspoons paprika

Directions

1. Preheat the Air fryer to 360 degrees F and grease an Air fryer basket.

2. Whisk eggs in a bowl and mix all the ingredients in another bowl except chicken pieces.

3. Dip the chicken in eggs and then coat generously with the dry mixture.

4. Arrange half of the chicken pieces in the Air fryer basket and cook for about 20 minutes.

5. Repeat with the remaining mixture and dish out to serve hot.

Nutrition:

Calories 218 kcal Carbs 2.6g Protein 27.9g

Creamy Chicken Tenders

Preparation Time: 15 minutes
Cooking Time: 20 minutes
Servings: 8

Ingredients:

- 2 pounds chicken tenders
- 1 cup feta cheese
- 4 tablespoons olive oil
- 1 cup cream
- Salt and black pepper, to taste

Directions

1. Preheat the Air fryer to 340 degrees F and grease an Air fryer basket.

2. Season the chicken tenders with salt and black pepper.

3. Arrange the chicken tenderloins in the Air fryer basket and drizzle with olive oil.\

4. Cook for about 15 minutes and set the Air fryer to 390 degrees F.

5. Cook for about 5 more minutes and dish out to serve warm.

6. Repeat with the remaining mixture and dish out to serve hot.

Nutrition:

Calories 344 kcal Carbs 1.7g Protein: 35.7g

Fried Chicken Thighs

Preparation Time: 10 minutes
Cooking Time: 25 minutes
Servings: 4

Ingredients:

- ½ cup almond flour
- 1 egg beaten
- 4 small chicken thighs
- 1½ tablespoons Old Bay Cajun Seasoning
- 1 teaspoon seasoning salt

Directions

1. Preheat the Air fryer to 380 degrees F for 3 minutes and grease an Air fryer basket.
2. Whisk the egg in a shallow bowl and place the old bay, flour and salt in another bowl.
3. Dip the chicken in the egg and coat with the flour mixture.
4. Arrange the chicken thighs in the Air fryer basket and cook for about 25 minutes.
5. Dish out in a platter and serve warm.

Nutrition:

Calories 180 kcal Carbs 3g Protein 21g

Vegetarian

Tangy Mushroom Pizza

Preparation time: 8-10 minutes
Cooking Time: 8 minutes
Number of Servings: 3-4

Ingredients:

- 3 tablespoons olive oil
- 3 cleaned portabella mushroom caps, scooped
- 3 tablespoons tomato sauce
- 12 slices pepperoni
- 3 tablespoons mozzarella, shredded
- 1 pinch salt
- 1 pinch dried Italian seasoning

Directions

1. Place your air fryer on a flat kitchen surface; plug it and turn it on. Set temperature to 330 degrees F and let it preheat for 4-5 minutes.
2. Take out the air-frying basket and gently coat it using a cooking oil or spray.
3. Now take the mushrooms and spread oil over them. On their inner side, add the Italian seasoning and salt. Top with the tomato sauce and cheese.
4. Add the mushrooms in the basket. Push the air-frying basket in the air fryer. Cook for 2 minutes.
5. Slide out the basket; add the slices of pepperoni and cook for 4-5 more minutes. Top with red pepper flakes and more cheese (optional).

Nutrition:

Calories 153 kcal Carbs 5.1g Protein – 5.4g

Mozzarella Radish Salad

Preparation time: 8-10 minutes
Cooking Time: 30 minutes
Number of Servings: 4

Ingredients:

- 1 ½ pounds radishes, trimmed and halved
- 2 tablespoons olive oil
- Pepper and salt, as needed

For the Salad:

- 1 teaspoon olive oil
- 1 tablespoon balsamic vinegar
- ½ pound mozzarella, sliced
- 1 teaspoon honey
- Pepper and salt, as needed

Directions

1. In a bowl of medium size, thoroughly mix the radishes, salt, black pepper, and oil.

2. Place your air fryer on a flat kitchen surface; plug it and turn it on. Set temperature to 350 degrees F and let it preheat for 4-5 minutes.

3. Add the mixture to the basket. Push the air-frying basket in the air fryer. Cook for 3 minutes.

4. In a bowl of medium size, thoroughly mix the fried radish and cheese.

5. In a bowl of small size, thoroughly mix the other ingredients and serve over the salad!

Nutrition:

Calories 363 kcal Carbs 4g Protein 2g

Buffalo Cauliflower

Preparation Time: 10 minutes
Cooking Time: 25 Minutes
Servings: 3-4

Ingredients:

- 2-3 tablespoons of hot sauce
- 1½ teaspoons of pure maple syrup
- 2 teaspoons of avocado oil
- 2-3 tablespoons of nutritional yeast
- ¼ teaspoon of sea salt
- 1 tablespoon of cornstarch
- 6 cups of ½ "cauliflower florets

Directions

1. Place the air fryer to 360 degrees F.

2. Add the hot sauce, maple syrup, avocado oil, nutritional yeast, sea salt, and cornstarch to a large-size bowl. Whisk well to incorporate fully.

3. Add the cauliflower florets and toss to coat well and evenly.

4. Add approximately half of the florets to your air fryer basket.

5. Cook in the air fryer for 12-14 minutes, shaking the basket halfway through cooking until the florets are your preferred consistency.

6. Repeat the process with the remaining cauliflower florets, for 8-10 minutes.

Nutrition:

Calories kcal 187 Carbs 3g Protein 15g Sugar 2g

Buttermilk Fried Mushrooms

Preparation Time: 5 minutes
Cooking Time: 45 Minutes
Servings: 2
Ingredients:

- 2 cups of cleaned oyster mushrooms
- 1 cup of buttermilk
- 1½ cups of all-purpose flour
- 1 teaspoon of salt
- 1 teaspoon of black pepper
- 1 teaspoon of garlic powder
- 1 teaspoon of onion powder
- 1 teaspoon of smoked paprika
- 1 teaspoon of cumin
- 1 tablespoon of oil

Directions:

1. Preheat your air fryer to 375 degrees.
2. Toss the mushrooms with the buttermilk and set aside to marinate for 15 minutes.
3. In a second larger bowl, combine the flour with the salt, pepper, garlic powder, onion powder, smoked paprika, cumin, and oil.
4. Take the mushrooms out of the buttermilk, setting the buttermilk to one side.
5. Dip each mushroom in the flour mixture, shaking off any excess flour. Dip the mushrooms once again in the buttermilk, then once again in the flour.
6. Liberally grease the bottom of the air fryer pan.
7. In a single layer, allowing space between the mushrooms, add the mushrooms to the pan. Cook for 5 minutes, before brushing them all over with a drop of oil.
8. Continue to cook for an additional 5-10 minutes, until crisp and golden.

Nutrition: Calories 602 kcal Carbs 3.1 Protein 24g

Lemon Broccoli

Preparation time: 10 minutes
Cooking time: 10 to 14 minutes
Servings 4

Ingredients:

- 1 large head fresh broccoli
- 2 teaspoons olive oil
- 1 tablespoon freshly squeezed lemon juice

Directions

1. Rinse the broccoli and pat dry. Cut off the florets and separate them.

2. Toss the broccoli, lemon juice, and olive oil until coated.

3. Roast the broccoli, in batches, at 380°F (193°C) for 10 to 14 minutes or until the broccoli is crisp-tender and slightly brown around the edges. Repeat with the remaining broccoli. Serve immediately.

Nutrition:

Calories 64 kcal Protein 4g Carbs 10g

Garlic Roasted Bell Peppers

Preparation time: 10 minutes
Cooking time: 18 to 20 minutes
Servings 4

Ingredients:

- 4 bell peppers, any colors, stemmed, seeded, membranes removed, and cut into fourths
- 1 teaspoon olive oil
- 4 garlic cloves, minced
- ½ teaspoon dried thyme

Directions

1. Place the peppers into the air fryer basket and drizzle with the olive oil. Toss gently. Roast at 350°F (177°C) for 15 minutes.

2. Sprinkle with the garlic and thyme. Roast for 3 to 5 minutes. Serve immediately.

Nutrition:

Calories 37 kcal Protein 1g Carbs 5g

Brussels Sprouts Curry

Preparation time: 13 minutes
Cooking time: 15 to 17 minutes
Servings 4

Ingredients:

- 1-pound (454 g) Brussels sprouts, ends trimmed, discolored leaves removed, and halved lengthwise
- 2 teaspoons olive oil
- 3 teaspoons curry powder, divided
- 1 tablespoon freshly squeezed lemon juice

Directions

1. Toss the Brussels sprouts with the olive oil and 1 teaspoon of curry powder. Transfer to the air fryer basket. Roast at 390°F (199°C) for 12 minutes, shaking the basket once during cooking.
2. Sprinkle with the remaining 2 teaspoons of the curry powder and the lemon juice. Shake again. Roast for another 5-7 minutes. Serve immediately.

Nutrition:

Calories 87 kcal Protein 4g Carbs 12g

Garlic Asparagus

Preparation time: 5 minutes
Cooking time: 4 to 5 minutes
Servings 4

Ingredients:

- 1-pound (454 g) asparagus, rinsed and ends trimmed
- 2 teaspoons olive oil
- 3 garlic cloves, minced
- 2 tablespoons balsamic vinegar
- ½ teaspoon dried thyme

Directions:

1. Toss the asparagus with the olive oil. Transfer to the air fryer basket.

2. Sprinkle with garlic. Roast at 380°F (193°C) for 4 to 5 minutes for crisp-tender or for 8 to 11 minutes for asparagus that is crisp on the outside and tender on the inside.

3. Drizzle with the balsamic vinegar and sprinkle with the thyme leaves. Serve immediately.

Nutrition:

Calories 42 kcal Protein 3g Carbs 6g

Honey-Glazed Carrots and Sweet Potato

Preparation time: 5 minutes
Cooking time: 20 to 25 minutes
Servings 4

Ingredients:

- 2 large carrots, cut into chunks
- 1 peeled and cut into 1-inch cubes medium sweet potato
- ½ cup chopped onion
- 2 garlic cloves, minced
- 2 tablespoons honey
- 1 tablespoon freshly squeezed orange juice
- 2 teaspoons butter, melted

Directions:

1. In a baking pan, toss the carrots, sweet potato, onion, garlic, honey, orange juice, and butter to coat.

2. Roast at 380°F (204°C) for 15 minutes. Check the vegetables. Shake the basket and roast for 5 to 10 minutes more, or until the vegetables are tender and glazed. Serve immediately.

Nutrition:

Calories 106 kcal Protein 1g Carbs 21g

Lemon Pepper Green Beans

Preparation time: 5 minutes
Cooking time: 10 minutes
Servings 2 cups

Ingredients:

- 2 cups fresh green beans
- 2 tablespoons olive oil
- 2 teaspoons granulated garlic
- ½ teaspoon salt
- ½ teaspoon lemon pepper

Directions

1. Trim the ends off of the green beans, and snap them in half.

2. In a large bowl, toss the beans in the olive oil, garlic, salt, and lemon pepper to coat.

3. Transfer the green beans to the air fryer basket and bake at 370°F (188°C) for 10 minutes, stopping halfway through to remove the basket and toss the green beans using a set of tongs.

4. Return the basket to the air fryer to continue baking for the remaining 5 minutes, or until the beans are fork tender, and serve.

Nutrition:

Calories 83 kcal Protein 1g Carbs 4g

Butter-Fried Plantains

Preparation time: 10 minutes
Cooking time: 8 minutes
Servings: 2

Ingredients:

- 2 ripe plantains, peeled and cut at a diagonal into ½-inch-thick pieces
- 3 tablespoons butter, melted
- ¼ teaspoon kosher salt

Directions

1. Toss the plantains with the butter and salt.

2. Arrange the plantain pieces in the air fryer basket. Air fry at 380°F (204°C) for 8 minutes. The plantains are done when they are soft and tender on the inside, and have plenty of crisp, sweet, brown spots on the outside. (The riper the plantains, the faster they will cook.)

Nutrition:

calories: 398 | fat: 18g | protein: 2g | carbs: 57g | fiber: 4g | sugar: 26g | sodium: 300mg

Goat Cheese Mixed Mushrooms

Preparation time: 10 minutes
Cooking time: 10 minutes
Servings: 4

Ingredients:

- 3 tablespoons vegetable oil
- 1 pound (454 g) mixed mushrooms, trimmed and sliced
- 1 clove garlic, minced
- ¼ teaspoon dried thyme
- ½ teaspoon black pepper
- 4 ounces (113 g) goat cheese, diced
- 2 teaspoons chopped fresh thyme leaves (optional)

Directions

1. In a baking pan, combine the oil, mushrooms, garlic, dried thyme, and pepper. Stir in the goat cheese.

2. Place in the air fryer basket. Roast at 380°F (204°C) for 10 minutes, stirring halfway through the cooking time.

3. Sprinkle with fresh thyme, if desired.

Nutrition:

Calories 248 kcal Protein 12g Carbs 5g

Air Fryer Radishes O'Brien

Preparation time: 10 minutes
Cooking time: 23 minutes
Servings 4

Ingredients:

- 2½ cups whole radishes, trimmed and each cut into 8 wedges
- 1 medium yellow or white onion, diced
- 1 small green bell pepper, stemmed, seeded, and diced
- 4 to 6 cloves garlic, thinly sliced
- ½ to 1 teaspoon kosher salt
- ½ to 1 teaspoon black pepper
- 2 tablespoons coconut oil, melted

Directions

1. Combine the radishes, onion, bell pepper, garlic, salt, and pepper. Pour the melted oil over the vegetables and mix well to coat.

2. Scrape the vegetables into the air fryer basket. Roast at 350°F (177°C) for 20 minutes. Increase the temperature to 380°F (204°C) and roast for 3 minutes to crisp up the edges of the vegetables. Serve hot.

Nutrition:

Calories 95 kcal Protein 1g Carbs 7g

Snacks

Pork Bites

Preparation time: 10 minutes
Cooking time: 15 minutes
Servings: 4

Ingredients:

- 2 teaspoons garlic powder
- 2 eggs
- Salt and black pepper to taste
- ¾ cup panko breadcrumbs
- ¾ cup coconut, shredded
- A drizzle of olive oil
- 1 pound ground pork

Directions

1. In a bowl, mix coconut with panko and stir well.

2. In another bowl, mix the pork, salt, pepper, eggs, and garlic powder, and then shape medium meatballs out of this mix.

3. Dredge the meatballs in the coconut mix, place them in your air fryer's basket, introduce in the air fryer, and cook at 350 degrees F for 15 minutes.

Nutrition:

Calories 192 kcal Carbs 14g. Protein 6 g.

Banana Chips

Preparation time: 5 minutes
Cooking time: 5 minutes
Servings: 8

Ingredients:

- ¼ cup peanut butter, soft
- 1 banana, peeled and sliced into 16 pieces
- 1 tablespoon vegetable oil

Directions

1. Put the banana slices in your air fryer's basket and drizzle the oil over them.

2. Cook at 360 degrees F for 5 minutes.

3. Transfer to bowls and serve them dipped in peanut butter.

Nutrition:

Calories 100 kcal Carbs 10g. Protein 4 g.

Lemony Apple Bites

Preparation time: 5 minutes
Cooking time: 5 minutes
Servings: 4

Ingredients:

- 3 big apples, cored, peeled and cubed
- 2 teaspoons lemon juice
- ½ cup caramel sauce

Directions

1. In your air fryer, mix all the ingredients; toss well.

2. Cook at 340 degrees F for 5 minutes.

3. Divide into cups and serve as a snack.

Nutrition:

Calories 180 kcal Carbs 10 g. Protein 3 g.

Zucchini Balls

Preparation time: 10 minutes
Cooking time: 12 minutes
Servings: 8

Ingredients:

- Cooking spray
- ½ cup dill, chopped
- 1 egg
- ½ cup white flour
- Salt and black pepper to taste
- 2 garlic cloves, minced
- 3 zucchinis, grated

Directions

1. In a bowl, mix all the ingredients and stir.

2. Shape the mix into medium balls and place them into your air fryer's basket.

3. Cook at 375 degrees F for 12 minutes, flipping them halfway.

4. Serve them as a snack right away.

Nutrition:

Calories 120 kcal Carbs 5g. Protein 3g.

Basil and Cilantro Crackers

Preparation time: 10 minutes
Cooking time: 16 minutes
Servings: 6

Ingredients:

- ½ teaspoon baking powder
- Salt and black pepper to taste
- 1¼ cups flour
- 1 garlic clove, minced
- 2 tablespoons basil, minced
- 2 tablespoons cilantro, minced
- 4 tablespoons butter, melted

Directions:

1. Add all of the ingredients to a bowl and stir until you obtain a dough.

2. Spread this on a lined baking sheet that fits your air fryer.

3. Place the baking sheet in the fryer at 325 degrees F and cook for 16 minutes.

4. Cool down, cut, and serve.

Nutrition:

Calories 171 kcal Carbs 8 g. Protein 4 g.

Balsamic Zucchini Slices

Preparation time: 5 minutes
Cooking time: 50 minutes
Servings: 6

Ingredients:

- 3 zucchinis, thinly sliced
- Salt and black pepper to taste
- 2 tablespoons avocado oil
- 2 tablespoons balsamic vinegar

Directions

1. Add all of the ingredients to a bowl and mix.

2. Put the zucchini mixture in your air fryer's basket and cook at 220 degrees F for 50 minutes.

3. Serve as a snack and enjoy!

Nutrition:

Calories 40 kcal Carbs 3g.Protein 7 g.

Turmeric Carrot Chips

Preparation time: 5 minutes
Cooking time: 25 minutes
Servings: 4

Ingredients:

- 4 carrots, thinly sliced
- Salt and black pepper to taste
- ½ teaspoon turmeric powder
- ½ teaspoon chaat masala
- 1 teaspoon olive oil

Directions:

1. Place all ingredients in a bowl and toss well.
2. Put the mixture in your air fryer's basket and cook at 370 degrees F for 25 minutes, shaking the fryer from time to time.
3. Serve as a snack.

Nutrition:

Calories 161 kcal Carbs 5 g.Protein 3 g.

Chives Radish Snack

Preparation time: 5 minutes
Cooking time: 10 minutes
Servings: 4

Ingredients:

- 16 radishes, sliced
- A drizzle of olive oil
- Salt and black pepper to taste
- 1 tablespoon chives, chopped

Directions

1. In a bowl, mix the radishes, salt, pepper, and oil; toss well.
2. Place the radishes in your air fryer's basket and cook at 350 degrees F for 10 minutes.
3. Divide into bowls and serve with chives sprinkled on top.

Nutrition:

Calories 100 kcal Carbs 4g. Protein 1 g.

Lentils Snack

Preparation time: 5 minutes
Cooking time: 12 minutes
Servings: 4

Ingredients:

- 15 ounces canned lentils, drained
- ½ teaspoon cumin, ground
- 1 tablespoon olive oil
- 1 teaspoon sweet paprika
- Salt and black pepper to taste

Directions

1. Place all ingredients in a bowl and mix well.
2. Transfer the mixture to your air fryer and cook at 380 degrees F for 12 minutes.
3. Divide into bowls and serve as a snack -or a side, or appetizer!.

Nutrition:

Calories 151 kcal Carbs 10g. Protein 6 g.

Air Fried Corn

Preparation time: 5 minutes
Cooking time: 10 minutes
Servings: 4

Ingredients:

- 2 tablespoons corn kernels
- 2½ tablespoons butter

Directions:

1. In a pan that fits your air fryer, mix the corn with the butter.

2. Place the pan in the fryer and cook at 380 degrees F for 10 minutes.

3. Serve as a snack and enjoy!

Nutrition:

Calories 70 kcal Carbs 7g. Protein 3g.

Salmon Tarts

Preparation time: 10 minutes
Cooking Time: 20 min
Servings: 15

Ingredients:

- 15 mini tart cases
- 4 eggs, lightly beaten
- ½ cup heavy cream
- Salt and black pepper
- 3 oz. smoked salmon
- 6 oz. cream cheese, divided into 15 pieces
- 6 fresh dill

Directions

1. Mix together eggs and cream in a pourable measuring container. Arrange the tarts into the air fryer. Pour in mixture into the tarts, about halfway up the side and top with a piece of salmon and a piece of cheese. Cook for 10 minutes at 340 F, regularly check to avoid overcooking. Sprinkle dill and serve chilled.

Nutrition:

Calories 415 kcal Carbs 43gProtein: 10g

Parmesan Crusted Pickles

Preparation time: 10 minutes
Cooking Time: 35 min
Servings: 4

Ingredients:

- 3 cups Dill Pickles, sliced, drained
- 2 eggs
- 2 tsp. water
- 1 cup Grated Parmesan cheese
- 1 ½ cups breadcrumbs, smooth
- black pepper to taste
- Cooking spray

Directions

1. Add the breadcrumbs and black pepper to a bowl and mix well; set aside. In another bowl, crack the eggs and beat with the water. Set aside. Add the cheese to a separate bowl; set aside. Preheat the Air Fryer to 380 F.

2. Pull out the fryer basket and spray it lightly with cooking spray. Dredge the pickle slices it in the egg mixture, then in breadcrumbs and then in cheese. Place them in the fryer without overlapping.

3. Slide the fryer basket back in and cook for 4 minutes. Turn them and cook for further for 5 minutes, until crispy. Serve with a cheese dip.

Nutrition:

Calories 335 kcal Carbs 34g Protein 17g

Breaded Mushrooms

Preparation time: 10 minutes
Cooking Time: 55 min
Servings: 4

Ingredients

- 1 lb. small Button mushrooms, cleaned
- 2 cups breadcrumbs
- 2 eggs, beaten
- Salt and pepper to taste
- 2 cups Parmigiano Reggiano cheese, grated

Directions

1. Preheat the Air Fryer to 360 F. Pour the breadcrumbs in a bowl, add salt and pepper and mix well. Pour the cheese in a separate bowl and set aside. Dip each mushroom in the eggs, then in the crumbs, and then in the cheese.

2. Slide out the fryer basket and add 6 to 10 mushrooms. Cook them for 20 minutes, in batches, if needed. Serve with cheese dip.

Nutrition:

Calories 487 kcal Carbs 49g Protein 31g

Cheesy Sticks with Sweet Thai Sauce

Preparation time: 10 minutes
Cooking Time: 2 hrs. 20 min
Servings: 4

Ingredients:

- 12 mozzarella string cheese
- 2 cups breadcrumbs
- 3 eggs
- 1 cup sweet Thai sauce
- 4 tbsp. skimmed milk

Directions

1. Pour the crumbs in a medium bowl. Crack the eggs into another bowl and beat with the milk. One after the other, dip each cheese sticks in the egg mixture, in the crumbs, then egg mixture again and then in the crumbs again.

2. Place the coated cheese sticks on a cookie sheet and freeze for 1 to 2 hours. Preheat the Air Fryer to 380 F. Arrange the sticks in the fryer without overcrowding. Cook for 5 minutes, flipping them halfway through cooking to brown evenly. Cook in batches. Serve with a sweet Thai sauce.

Nutrition:

Calories 158 kcal Carbs 14g Protein 9g

Bacon Wrapped Avocados

Preparation time: 10 minutes
Cooking Time: 40 min
Servings: 6

Ingredients

- 12 thick strips bacon
- 3 large avocados, sliced
- 1/3 tsp. salt
- 1/3 tsp. chili powder
- 1/3 tsp. cumin powder

Directions

1. Stretch the bacon strips to elongate and use a knife to cut in half to make 24 pieces. Wrap each bacon piece around a slice of avocado from one end to the other end. Tuck the end of bacon into the wrap. Arrange on a flat surface and season with salt, chili and cumin on both sides.

2. Arrange 4 to 8 wrapped pieces in the fryer and cook at 350 F for 8 minutes, or until the bacon is browned and crunchy, flipping halfway through to cook evenly. Remove onto a wire rack and repeat the process for the remaining avocado pieces.

Nutrition:

Calories 193 kcal Carbs 10g Protein 4g

Hot Chicken Wingettes

Preparation time: 10 minutes
Cooking Time: 45 min
Servings: 3

Ingredients

- 15 chicken wingettes
- Salt and pepper to taste
- 1/3 cup hot sauce
- 1/3 cup butter
- ½ tbsp. vinegar

Directions

1. Preheat the Air Fryer to 360 F. Season the wingettes with pepper and salt. Add them to the air fryer and cook for 35 minutes. Toss every 5 minutes. Once ready, remove them into a bowl. Over low heat, melt the butter in a saucepan. Add the vinegar and hot sauce. Stir and cook for a minute.

2. Turn the heat off. Pour the sauce over the chicken. Toss to coat well. Transfer the chicken to a serving platter. Serve with a side of celery strips and blue cheese dressing.

Nutrition:

Calories 563 kcal Carbs 2g Protein 35g

Mouth-Watering Salami Sticks

Preparation time: 10 minutes
Cooking Time: 2 hrs. 10 min
Servings: 3

Ingredients:

- 1 lb. ground beef
- 3 tbsp. sugar
- A pinch garlic powder
- A pinch chili powder
- Salt to taste
- 1 tsp. liquid smoke

Directions

1. Place the meat, sugar, garlic powder, chili powder, salt and liquid smoke in a bowl. Mix with a spoon. Mold out 4 sticks with your hands, place them on a plate, and refrigerate for 2 hours. Cook at 350 F. for 10 minutes, flipping once halfway through.

Nutrition:

Calories 428 kcal Carbs 12g Protein 42g

Carrot Crisps

Preparation time: 10 minutes
Cooking Time: 20 min
Servings: 2

Ingredients

- 3 large carrots, washed and peeled
- Salt to taste
- Cooking spray

Directions

2. Using a mandolin slicer, slice the carrots very thinly height wise. Put the carrot strips in a bowl and season with salt to taste. Grease the fryer basket lightly with cooking spray, and add the carrot strips. Cook at 350 F for 10 minutes, stirring once halfway through.

Nutrition:

Calories 35 kcal Carbs 8g Protein 1g

Calamari with Olives

Preparation time: 10 minutes
Cooking Time: 25 min
Servings: 3

Ingredients

- ½ lb. calamari rings
- ½ piece coriander, chopped
- 2 strips chili pepper, chopped
- 1 tbsp. olive oil
- 1 cup pimiento-stuffed green olives, sliced
- Salt and black pepper to taste

Directions

1. In a bowl, add rings, chili pepper, salt, black pepper, oil, and coriander. Mix and let marinate for 10 minutes. Pour the calamari into an oven-safe bowl that fits into the fryer basket.

2. Slide the fryer basket out, place the bowl in it, and slide the basket back in. Cook for 15 minutes stirring every 5 minutes using a spoon, at 400 F. After 15 minutes, and add in the olives.

3. Stir, close and continue to cook for 3 minutes. Once ready, transfer to a serving platter. Serve warm with a side of bread slices and mayonnaise.

Nutrition:

Calories 128 kcal Carbs 10g Protein 22g

Sweet Mixed Nuts

Preparation time: 10 minutes
Cooking Time: 25 min
Servings: 5

Ingredients

- ½ cup pecans
- ½ cup walnuts
- ½ cup almonds
- A pinch cayenne pepper
- 2 tbsp. sugar
- 2 tbsp. egg whites
- 2 tsp. cinnamon
- Cooking spray

Directions

1. Add the pepper, sugar, and cinnamon to a bowl and mix well; set aside. In another bowl, mix in the pecans, walnuts, almonds, and egg whites. Add the spice mixture to the nuts and give it a good mix. Lightly grease the fryer basket with cooking spray.

2. Pour in the nuts, and cook them for 10 minutes. Stir the nuts using a wooden vessel, and cook for further for 10 minutes. Pour the nuts in the bowl. Let cool before crunching on them.

Nutrition:

Calories 147 kcal Carbs 10g Protein 3g

Desserts

Easy Cheesecake

Preparation time: 10 minutes
Cooking time: 25 Minutes
Servings: 15

Ingredients:

- 1 lb. cream cheese
- 1/2 tsp. vanilla extract
- 1 cup graham crackers; crumbled
- 2 tbsp. butter
- 2 eggs
- 4 tbsp. sugar

Directions:

1. In a bowl; mix crackers with butter.
2. Press crackers mix on the bottom of a lined cake pan, introduce in your air fryer and cook at 350 °F, for 4 minutes
3. Meanwhile; in a bowl, mix sugar with cream cheese, eggs and vanilla and whisk well.
4. Spread filling over crackers crust and cook your cheesecake in your air fryer at 310 °F, for 15 minutes. Leave cake in the fridge for 3 hours, slice and serve

Nutrition: Calories 245 kcal Carbs 20g.Protein 3g.

Macaroons

Preparation time: 10 minutes
Cooking time: 18 Minutes
Servings: 20

Ingredients:

- 2 tbsp. sugar
- 2 cup coconut; shredded
- 4 egg whites
- 1 tsp. vanilla extract

Directions:

1. In a bowl; mix egg whites with stevia and beat using your mixer

2. Add coconut and vanilla extract, whisk again, shape small balls out of this mix, introduce them in your air fryer and cook at 340 °F, for 8 minutes. Serve macaroons cold

Nutrition:

Calories 55kcal Carbs 2 g. Protein 1 g.

Bread Dough and Amaretto Dessert

Preparation time: 10 minutes
Cooking time: 22 Minutes
Servings: 12

Ingredients:

- 1 lb. bread dough
- 1 cup heavy cream
- 12 oz. chocolate chips
- 1 cup sugar
- 1/2 cup butter; melted
- 2 tbsp. amaretto liqueur

Directions:

1. Roll dough, cut into 20 slices and then cut each slice in halves.

2. Brush dough pieces with butter, sprinkle sugar, place them in your air fryer's basket after you've brushed it some butter, cook them at 350 °F, for 5 minutes; flip them, cook for 3 minutes more and transfer to a platter

3. Heat up a pan with the heavy cream over medium heat, add chocolate chips and stir until they melt. Add liqueur; stir again, transfer to a bowl and serve bread dippers with this sauce

Nutrition:

Calories 200 kcal Carbs 6g. Protein 6 g.

Banana Bread

Preparation time: 10 minutes
Cooking time: 50 Minutes
Servings: 6

Ingredients:

- 3/4 cup sugar
- 1/3 cup butter
- 1/3 cup milk
- 1 tsp. vanilla extract
- 1 egg
- 2 bananas; mashed
- 1 tsp. baking powder
- 1 ½ cups flour
- 1/2 tsp. baking soda
- 1 ½ tsp. cream of tartar
- Cooking spray

Directions:

1. In a bowl; mix milk with cream of tartar, sugar, butter, egg, vanilla and bananas and stir everything.
2. In another bowl, mix flour with baking powder and baking soda
3. Combine the 2 mixtures; stir well, pour this into a cake pan greased with some cooking spray, introduce in your air fryer and cook at 320 °F, for 40 minutes. Take bread out, leave aside to cool down, slice and serve it.

Nutrition:

Calories 292 kcal Carbs 28g.Protein 4 g.

Easy Granola

Preparation time: 10 minutes
Cooking time: 45 Minutes
Servings: 4

Ingredients:

- 1 cup coconut; shredded
- 1/2 cup almonds
- 1/2 cup pecans; chopped.
- 2 tbsp. sugar
- 1/2 cup pumpkin seeds
- 1/2 cup sunflower seeds
- 2 tbsp. sunflower oil
- 1 tsp. nutmeg; ground
- 1 tsp. apple pie spice mix

Directions

1. In a bowl; mix almonds and pecans with pumpkin seeds, sunflower seeds, coconut, nutmeg and apple pie spice mix and stir well

2. Heat up a pan with the oil over medium heat, add sugar and stir well.

3. Pour this over nuts and coconut mix and stir well

4. Spread this on a lined baking sheet that fits your air fryer, introduce in your air fryer and cook at 300 °F and bake for 25 minutes. Leave your granola to cool down, cut and serve.

Nutrition:

Calories 322 kcal Carbs 12g.Protein 7 g.

Banana Cake

Preparation time: 10 minutes
Cooking time: 40 Minutes
Servings: 4

Ingredients:

- 1 tbsp. butter; soft
- 1 egg
- 1/3 cup brown sugar
- 1 tsp. baking powder
- 1/2 tsp. cinnamon powder
- 2 tbsp. honey
- 1 banana; peeled and mashed
- 1 cup white flour
- Cooking spray

Directions:

1. Spray a cake pan with some cooking spray and leave aside.

2. In a bowl; mix butter with sugar, banana, honey, egg, cinnamon, baking powder and flour and whisk

3. Pour this into a cake pan greased with cooking spray, introduce in your air fryer and cook at 350 °F, for 30 minutes. Leave cake to cool down, slice and serve

Nutrition:

Calories 232 kcal Carbs 34g. Protein 4g.

Fried Bananas

Preparation time: 10 minutes
Cooking time: 25 Minutes
Servings: 4

Ingredients:

- 3 tbsp. butter
- 3 tbsp. cinnamon sugar
- 1 cup panko
- 2 eggs
- 8 bananas; peeled and halved
- 1/2 cup corn flour

Directions

1. Heat up a pan with the butter over medium high heat, add panko; stir and cook for 4 minutes and then transfer to a bowl

2. Roll each in flour, eggs and panko mix, arrange them in your air fryer's basket, dust with cinnamon sugar and cook at 280 °F, for 10 minutes. Serve right away.

Nutrition:

Calories 164 kcal Carbs 32 g. Protein 4 g.

Tomato Cake

Preparation time: 10 minutes
Cooking time: 40 Minutes
Servings: 4

Ingredients:

- 1 ½ cups flour
- 1 tsp. cinnamon powder
- 1 cup tomatoes chopped
- 1/2 cup olive oil
- 1 tsp. baking powder
- 1 tsp. baking soda
- 3/4 cup maple syrup
- 2 tbsp. apple cider vinegar

Directions

1. In a bowl; mix flour with baking powder, baking soda, cinnamon and maple syrup and stir well.

2. In another bowl, mix tomatoes with olive oil and vinegar and stir well

3. Combine the 2 mixtures; stir well, pour into a greased round pan that fits your air fryer, introduce in the fryer and cook at 360 °F, for 30 minutes. Leave cake to cool down, slice and serve.

Nutrition:

Calories 153 kcal Carbs 25g. Protein 4g.

Pumpkin Cookies

Preparation time: 10 minutes
Cooking time: 25 Minutes
Servings: 24

Ingredients:

- 2 ½ cups flour
- 1/2 tsp. baking soda
- 2 tbsp. butter
- 1 tsp. vanilla extract
- 1 tbsp. flax seed; ground
- 3 tbsp. water
- 1/2 cup pumpkin flesh; mashed
- 1/4 cup honey
- 1/2 cup dark chocolate chips

Directions

1. In a bowl; mix flax seed with water; stir and leave aside for a few minutes.

2. In another bowl, mix flour with salt and baking soda

3. In a third bowl, mix honey with pumpkin puree, butter, vanilla extract and flaxseed.

4. Combine flour with honey mix and chocolate chips and stir

5. Scoop 1 tbsp. of cookie dough on a lined baking sheet that fits your air fryer, repeat with the rest of the dough, introduce them in your air fryer and cook at 350 °F, for 15 minutes.

6. Leave cookies to cool down and serve.

Nutrition:

Calories 140 kcal Carbs 17g. Protein 10g.

Apple Bread

Preparation time: 10 minutes
Cooking time: 50 Minutes
Servings: 6

Ingredients:

- 3 cups apples; cored and cubed
- 1 cup sugar
- 1 tbsp. baking powder
- 1 stick butter
- 1 tbsp. vanilla
- 2 eggs
- 1 tbsp. apple pie spice
- 2 cups white flour
- 1 cup water

Directions

1. In a bowl mix egg with 1 butter stick, apple pie spice and sugar and stir using your mixer.
2. Add apples and stir again well
3. In another bowl, mix baking powder with flour and stir.
4. Combine the 2 mixtures; stir and pour into a spring form pan
5. Put spring form pan in your air fryer and cook at 320 °F, for 40 minutes Slice and serve.

Nutrition:

Calories 192 kcal Carbs 14g. Protein 7g.

Bread Pudding

Preparation time: 10 minutes
Cooking time: 1 hour 10 Minutes
Servings: 4

Ingredients:

- 6 glazed doughnuts; crumbled
- 1 cup cherries
- 4 egg yolks
- 1/4 cup sugar
- 1/2 cup chocolate chips.
- 1 ½ cups whipping cream
- 1/2 cup raisins

Directions

1. In a bowl; mix cherries with egg yolks and whipping cream and stir well.

2. In another bowl, mix raisins with sugar, chocolate chips and doughnuts and stir

3. Combine the 2 mixtures, transfer everything to a greased pan that fits your air fryer and cook at 310 °F, for 1 hour. Chill pudding before cutting and serving it

Nutrition:

Calories 302 kcal Carbs 23g. Protein 10g.

Chocolate and Pomegranate Bars

Preparation time: 10 minutes
Cooking time: 2 hours 10 Minutes
Servings: 6

Ingredients:

- 1/2 cup milk
- 1/2 cup almonds; chopped
- 1 tsp. vanilla extract
- 1 ½ cups dark chocolate; chopped
- 1/2 cup pomegranate seeds

Directions:

1. Heat up a pan with the milk over medium low heat, add chocolate; stir for 5 minutes; take off heat add vanilla extract, half of the pomegranate seeds and half of the nuts and stir

2. Pour this into a lined baking pan, spread, sprinkle a pinch of salt, the rest of the pomegranate arils and nuts, introduce in your air fryer and cook at 300 °F, for 4 minutes. Keep in the fridge for 2 hours before serving.

Nutrition:

Calories 68 kcal Carbs 6g. Protein 1g.

Tips

Here are some tips you can use when cooking in an air fryer:

1) Cut vegetables into evenly sized pieces for even cooking results.

2) Place your ingredients one layer deep for even cooking.

3) Drizzle oils, dressings, or glazes over the top of your meal such as the sauce, butter, or seasoning sauces to keep it from sticking to the air fryer and produce a crispy exterior.

4) Cook at a lower temperature so that food doesn't burn on the outside before it's properly cooked inside.

5) When cooking meat, dredge it in flour or bread crumbs before placing it in the air fryer. This will ensure that the meat cooks all the way through and is moist.

6) Be sure to spray a non-stick cooking spray on your air fryer basket because sometimes there might be some foods sticking to it.

7) Make sure you're shaking up the basket from time to time while your food is cooking for more even browning/cooking.

8) Make sure to measure out your ingredients accordingly as this will help you get an even result.

9) The cooking temperature should be set at 380 degrees F to avoid burning your food.

Conclusion

Thank you for making it to the end. For culinary delight, some add seasoning or seasonings to their food and cook in an air fryer. To get the most out of an air fryer you will need to consider getting a unit that has a basket with a lid so you can ensure that the air circulates throughout. You can use an air fryer with a variety of foods. There are a lot of manufacturers who supply air fryers that are cheaply priced, providing many people with an opportunity to purchase them. Air frying foods is an easy and healthy way to cook your food and help you keep fit.

The air fryer is a new kitchen appliance that contains a basket that comes with a lid, making it possible for users to cook their food without the need of using oil or any type of fat. Cooking with an air fryer leaves less fat and calories in your food and eliminates the need for deep frying.

There are many benefits of cooking in an air fryer, including not having to use any fat or oil as it cooks. The food you cook will be very crispy because of the hot air circulating in the basket but you will not be cooking with oil or butter and the food will not absorb all those extra fats and oils. This means that your food is healthier to eat because you are cooking with less fat and calories. You can also consider using a source of oil that has a lower burning point than oil used for deep frying as this will help to ensure that your food does not burn and become overcooked by using an air fryer.

I hope you liked this book!

Printed in Great Britain
by Amazon